Let Us Pray

A Collection of Prayers For Worship

by

Bill Hughes

MOORLEY'S Print & Publishing

Revised and enlarged edition
© Copyright 2002

All rights reserved. No part of this publication may be reproduced, stored in a retrieval system, or transmitted, in any form or by any means, electronic, mechanical, photocopying, recording or otherwise, without the prior written permission of the publishers.

There is no restriction on the public reading of these prayers

British Library Cataloguing in Publication Data.
A catalogue record for this book is available from the British Library.

Original version of Let Us Pray © 1984
The Place of Prayer © 1980
The Door is Open © 1982

MOORLEY'S Print & Publishing
23 Park Rd., Ilkeston, Derbys DE7 5DA
Tel/Fax: (0115) 932 0643

ISBN 0 86071 548 5

Advent

Almighty God, we praise You that the whole of history was a preparation for Your coming to us in Jesus Christ.

You spoke through the prophets and have spoken to us in the saints of every age.

You speak so intimately to us in Jesus.

Speak with us in this time of worship. May Your Holy Spirit tune our hearts to sing with gladness the truths we believe.

Through Jesus Christ our Lord.
                Amen.

O Blessed God, as we prepare ourselves for the Advent of Your Son, our Saviour Jesus Christ, help us by Your Holy Spirit to do all that we do in gladness and love.

Keep us mindful of the spiritual realities that Jesus came to show us,

and help us to know that all life is sacred since He came,

and the whole of life a sacrament of praise and thanksgiving,

for we are daily in His company – everywhere.

Hear us for Jesus Christ's sake.
                Amen.

Christmas

Our Father God, we thank You for Your most gracious gift, in Jesus,
to an ungrateful race.
He came and still comes to us.
He speaks to us in a language that we can understand –
the language of love.
He calls, and we respond as did Peter and the others,
and He fulfils our deep desire for life that is victorious.
He empowers us to love and serve our fellows.
Help us this Christmastide to know His presence in our hearts
and in our homes.
For Your Name's sake.　　　　　　　　　　　　　　**Amen.**

O God, the Father of Jesus Christ, and ours, we give thanks for the birth of Jesus - Someone who we can see and know.

In Him You came to redeem us and set us free; to offer us the gift of newness of life.

As we take the Bethlehem Road again, help us to offer our adoration, and as the great day becomes a memory, and the mundane is with us once more, keep us rejoicing in all that we have seen and heard in this hour.

O Lord and Master, Jesus Christ, we bless You that You knew life as we know it - an earthly home, its joys and sorrows, its victories and its temptations: that in the home at Nazareth You learned obedience and trust.

Bless our homes; stay with us in the family, sharing our daily life.

Help us, by Your presence, to live at our best.

Rebuke us when we fail in love, are selfish and want our own way, or are irritable and spoil the lives of those we love.

LET US PRAY FOR

Those who will be separated from home and family at this time.

Our own family and friends.

Those on duty providing for our needs and comfort.

Those at sea, and in foreign ports.

Those serving in our forces overseas.

All missionaries, teachers, doctors, working among the poor and needy in other lands at the call of Jesus.

The homeless and refugees, remembering that our Lord had nowhere to lay His head.

Bless, Lord, we pray,

> all who have been bereft of loved ones since last Christmastide - and bless us, with happy hours, kind thoughts and rich memories and grateful hearts for all Your love.

Hear us, we pray. **Amen.**

At the Beginning of Another Year

O God our Father, we thank You - that we find ourselves again at the beginning of another year.

We thank You for joys and sorrows, laughter and tears;
> for silence and song, for through it all You have been loving us with an everlasting love.

We give thanks for times
> of gladness which will be to us for ever happy memories,
> for times of sorrow which drew us to Yourself;
> for successes which lit life with delight,
> and for failures which kept us humble.

Thank You, for the things which do not change,
> for the loyalty of friends,
> for the loved ones who are dearer to us with the passing years,
> and above all for Jesus Christ in whom we live to the uttermost, and who has made us rich by His grace.

But we pray for others too, at this hour,

Bless those for whom the days ahead will be lonelier, those from whom death has taken away someone dear to them; help them in spite of everything, to face life with steady eyes.

Bless those for whom life will be more difficult, whose illness has left them less able to face the strenuous demands of life.

We pray for those who, this new year, will have difficult decisions to make, when they stand at the cross roads, guide them and give them grace to follow Your leading.

Bless, O God, those who look forward to the year ahead,
> those hoping to complete some task or course of study;
> those who plan to marry.

And give to us all that sure faith in You, and the Spirit of Jesus, that we may know that we never walk alone.

Hear us for Jesus Christ's sake. **Amen.**

At the Beginning of Another Year (ii)

O God our Father, we thank You that You have brought us again to the beginning of another year.

We give thanks for joys and sorrows, laughter and tears, silence and song, for through it all You have been loving us with an everlasting love.

We thank You for times of gladness which will be to us forever, happy memories - for times of sorrow, which drove us to Yourself because there was nowhere else to go for comfort, healing and understanding, for in all our sorrows You too, sorrow.

We bless Your Holy Name for the things that do not change with the passing years - for the loyalty of friends, who are always the first to arrive in an emergency - and the last to go: for the loved ones who are dearer to us with the passing years, and above all for Jesus Christ, in whom we live to the uttermost and who has made us rich by His grace.

But, not for ourselves alone do we pray, Father, at this changing of the year; we pray for those who will be glad that a year is dying and a new one being born that they may begin again, leaving the failures of the past behind. Their longing seeks Your nearness - speak there, Lord.

Bless those for whom the days ahead will be lonelier, and help them, in spite of everything, to face life with steady eyes. We pray, for those for whom life will be more difficult - those whose illness has left them less able to face the strenuous demands of life. Bless those who look forward to the year ahead - those who have plans for their work, those who hope to complete some task or study.

Bless Your Church, give her gentleness of heart, certainty of faith, and strength of action.

Let us spend a moment in silence before God, confessing our sins and making any special request of Him.

Hear our prayers O God for Jesus' sake.
                                                                    Amen.

Epiphany

Wise men knelt in that stable, O God, before Your Son, our Saviour.

We are not wise or noble, but we know that Jesus is the Light of the world, that He sheds light upon many of the perplexities that are ours and that He is the light within our hearts,

so we bring Him now our grateful thanks and the overflowing of our adoration in our service for Your Kingdom;
through Jesus Christ our Lord. **Amen.**

The only journey we make to You, Lord Jesus, is from our sinfulness to Your redeeming love.

We have no star to guide us, but we have our great need.

So, we come now.

> Still our hearts, make us conscious of Your presence, draw us closer to Yourself.

Accept what we now give You, our praise and the gratitude of a thankful heart.

Amen.

Passion Sunday

O God, our Father, we give You thanks for the love shown to us in the Passion and Cross of our Lord and Saviour Jesus Christ - a love that will never give us up, and never let us go. We may stray from You, and You will seek us, coming to us in moments of kindness, the faithfulness of a friend - showing Yourself to us in the needs of another - those moments when our hearts are touched, and we know it is Yourself.

Forgive us, that like Peter, we have denied You. In an alien world, a world where it is too easy to go with the crowd, we have often lost our identity. We ought to have spoken, but remained silent because we were afraid. Forgive us, Lord, and in those moments of temptation, throw Your grace around us that we may be bold in proclaiming the Christian standard and the truth of the Gospel.

Thank You, Father for forgiveness! In the strength of grace we begin again, in the company of Jesus.

Bless, Father, those who have been broken by life - those whose circumstances always seem to be against them. Those who have never had good health. Those who suffer mental anguish and are full of remorse - help them to find in Jesus, the health and peace they desire.

Bless all in the local community who are in the service of their fellows - some known to us but many are not.

Bless all who will be on duty at their task whilst we sleep - those who walk the midnight wards of our hospitals, Emergency Services crews alert for an emergency call.

Give to us, Lord, a heart of compassion that we may comfort the sad, lift up the fallen, and seek the lost.

Hear us for Your Son, our Saviour's sake.

Amen.

Palm Sunday

O Lord Jesus Christ, we remember this day that You entered the city which refused to acknowledge You, and where, on a hill, they crucified You.
Enter into our hearts and subdue them to Yourself,
    And, as Your faithful disciples blessed Your coming and spread their garments in the way, make us ready to lay at Your feet all that we have and are.
We give thanks that You have reconciled us to Your Father, brought us out of our darkness into Your marvellous light so that we walk today in the fellowship of Your love.
Give us, Lord Jesus, the grace of humility –
    help us to realise our own ignorance, for there is much that we don't know –
    humility to forget ourselves, our rights, our prestige, for we have none if we are disciples of Yours –
    we are always servants, and slaves of righteousness.
Save us from all pride - the intellectual pride which despises the simple and uneducated - and from spiritual pride which makes us think ourselves better than others, and the arrogance of feeling that we have a monopoly of the truth.
We pray for our town, Lord, all in authority and whose task it is to look after the affairs of all our citizens.
For those in the field of education, and health, and those whose task is to keep it clean and tidy.
Our hospitals and staff, and our general practitioners.
We pray for all our citizens, those perplexed by mental problems or worried by personal problems.
    Those who are unhappy at home or at work.
Bless all our Churches and their ministers, quicken in us we pray a zeal for evangelism.
Renew within us, O Saviour, that life that You came to give abundantly, and send us out from this hour, in sacrificial service to all men.
For Your Name's sake. **Amen.**

Good Friday

O God, whose eternal love for our weak and struggling race has been shown to us in the blessed life and death of Jesus Christ our Saviour, enable us in this hour, to have fellowship with Him in His sorrow that we may learn the secret of His courage, steadfastness and peace.

May we be embraced in that great company whom no man can number - those to whom new life and power for living has come through Calvary. May the redeeming power that has flowed from His passion flow now into our souls.

We need forgiveness, Father.

We repent, now, of our sins - sins of the flesh and of the spirit, for it is the sins of the spirit to which we are most prone.
Like Your disciples of old, we too can betray love in the most subtle ways as Judas did.
We can deny our allegiance to You, as Peter did, because it may cost too much.

Forgive us, O God, and bid us go and sin no more.

And give to us, we pray the sensitive spirit - eyes to see the need and heart aches of others, to be angry at the injustices that men suffer, the inhumanities of life. Help us to sit where they sit and bring Your love and care into their situation.

Give to us the power of Your Holy Spirit to carry through the things to which we have committed ourselves, for so often we start well, but we fail to finish.

Grant help and healing to those upon whom life has placed an undeserved cross, the innocent who suffer along with the guilty, especially children from unloving homes, those who suffer because their partner is an alcoholic, those born with disabilities. Bless them all. Draw us closer to Jesus, that we may be closer to them.

Hear us, for Your love's sake.

Amen.

Easter Day

O Blessed God, all things conspire this morning to make us glad, new life is about us in garden and hedgerow, the birds sing praises. But above all, the glory of an endless world shines through from a spring of yesterday - an empty tomb in a garden, and Jesus Christ alive for evermore - the grim barred gates of death swung back and the Kingdom of Heaven is opened to all believers – Hallelujah!

We thank You, Father, for love and all that it means to us - that love that has been ours all our days - in family, in friends, in those who love us beyond our deserving and whose loss would cause us a sleepless night and a trance-like day.

We thank You for every remembrance of those who have joined the Church triumphant, they still influence our lives for good.

We thank You that we never walk alone, for the risen Jesus our Divine Companion leads and guides us, comforts and strengthens us.

We pray, O God, for those whose only knowledge of life is that of futility - nothing seems to add up, no one cares, they don't count.

For those whose dreams have faded and they are too old to start again.

Those to whom every day is the same and happy surprises never come;

for those whose hearts are bitter because they have been badly treated by another.

We pray for those who nurse a grudge against someone and know no spirit of forgiveness;

for all who seek peace and cannot find it.

On this glad Easter Day, when our hearts are filled to overflowing with Your grace, Lord Jesus, grant that these for whom we pray may know life victorious too.

Amen.

The Ascension

Almighty God, You have enriched our lives with countless blessings, guarded us continually by Your grace, and brought us again to this hour and this place.

We thank You for Your goodness which never fails.

We praise You for Jesus, who gave Himself for us on the Cross and now lives as King of earth and heaven.

We rejoice that He rules in our hearts and that this world is Your world and throughout it run Your purposes.

Guide us by Your Holy Spirit in this hour that we may know Your will for us, through Christ our Lord.

Amen.

We thank You, Father, for the glorified humanity of Jesus which through faith we are permitted to share.

We know that He ever lives to make intercession for us, and that He has gone to prepare a place for us in heaven.

We know that our wills are ours to make them Yours;

we pray, then, that our hearts may be lifted above all that is sinful, that we may possess the values of the Kingdom – righteousness and peace and joy in the Holy Spirit,

through Jesus Christ our Lord. **Amen.**

Whit Sunday

O God, here, in the Holy place, assembled together, of one accord, as those of old, we come to worship.

We come in the spirit of expectancy, reveal Yourself to our waiting hearts through Your Holy Spirit.

Open our hearts to the truth of Your word, enlarge our vision, give us peace and joy in believing, and then, send us out as witnesses to the life that is life indeed, that men may see in us a vitality that makes them wonder.

O Holy Spirit of God, who moved within our hearts to draw us to Jesus, who enlightened our minds, brought us out of the darkness into the light, maintain and increase, we pray, the gifts that are already ours that Your power may come upon Your Church and into the hearts of men that they too may live upon resources beyond their own.

Grant, we pray, that each of us may become an ambassador of the Good News in our business life, at the office, in the factory and workshop. Call us to the life of holiness, and a winsome discipleship.

Give to us that insight into the spiritual needs of those with whom we are in daily contact, and deliver us from self-consciousness in speaking of our conversion - give to us the moment, then the right word.

Lead us, Lord, in the fellowship here, into the lives of others with compassion, understanding and love. Hear us for the suffering, the anxious and afraid, especially any known to us; for all who tend the sick in our local hospitals. And in Your mercy, Lord, heal us all, in forgiveness and keep us near the Cross where burdens are lifted and burdens carried. In Jesus' name we ask these prayers.

Amen.

O Holy Spirit of God, the Lord and giver of life, by whom alone we come into the Kingdom of love, we thank You for Your Church, militant, upon earth and triumphant in heaven. Bless her throughout the world.

Especially would we pray for the young Church in difficult situations in other lands*　May she stand firm in the evil day, lead her into all the truth, refresh her with Your comfort, and give her a right judgement in all things. Hear us, for Jesus Christ's sake.

Amen.

* Include any current situation

Trinity Sunday

Let us thank God

For our knowledge of the Father, through the Son, and for our knowledge of the Son, through the ministry of the Holy Spirit.

Accept our thanks, most gracious God, for our new life in Jesus - our new perspective to life, our new attitude to our fellows and our new experience of the guided life through Your Holy Spirit.

Let us, in silence, make our confessions to God.

We confess, O God, our sins - the things we have done which were unworthy of a Christian - and the things that we know we ought to have done, but haven't. We excuse ourselves too much,

Lord, forgive us.

We confess our lack of the spirit of wonder - our intellectual pride which prevents us knowing Your truth which is only revealed to the humble.

Give to us that simplicity of heart that was in Jesus. Help us to grow in grace and the knowledge of Your beloved Son, our Saviour.

This day, especially, Father, we pray for Theologians and those in Theological Colleges. We pray that young men and women may hear Your call to the ministry.

We pray for all ministers of the Gospel. Bless, O God, Your servants everywhere, give them strength in difficult situations, and keep them humble when success attends their labours. Enable us, within this fellowship, to bear our witness to the light in a world of shadows and half-lights. Help us to treat all men with respect, to forgive when they wrong us, and to love them always.

Bless, O God those who are not far from the Kingdom - may the remembered word, or the remembered personality, touch a chord in a heart that is tender towards Jesus - lead them home.

Amen.

Education for Life
Mark 6: 1-6

O God, our Father, Creator of all that is, for the wonder and beauty of nature, our ability to see it, and for the depths of our spirit that it touches, we praise You.

We thank You for those moments when hills speak and trees whisper, and we are moved to worship. For those moments when the depths are reached - in the gladness, a child is born, or in sadness, someone dies.

We bless You for the created world, our creation, and our new creation in Jesus Christ.

We bless You for all that we have learned of Your love through others - those who taught us in early days, at home, in Sunday school, and Christian fellowships. We thank You for every remembrance of them, for their patience with some of us who were slow to learn, and their encouragement which helped us to try again.

We pray for all, who teach today - and all who learn, especially those known to us who teach, or learn, in School, College or University. Guide all young people and protect them in the difficulties and temptations which beset them in new surroundings away from home. Keep alive in their hearts the love of all that is good in their home life.

O Saviour Christ, who taught with authority – the authority of Your Father, help us, scholars in Your School, to learn the lesson of the Cross, that love always triumphs over wrong and can never fail. Teach us Your patience, for often we are bungling instruments of the kingdom, impatient with those who do not see as we see. Teach us, when things go wrong, that You have a plan for us in Your purpose, and in Your will is our peace and blessing. Give to us the child-like heart that trusts, believes and loves always, for Your name's sake. **Amen.**

Sunday School, Sunday Club Junior Church

O God our Father, we thank You for today, our anniversary Sunday. We are here as a family, young and old, glad to be together - teacher and scholar, and we are all learners in Your school of life.

Our hearts are glad because we know that You love us - Jesus told us so. You will be with us always, in hard days and easy ones, in storm and sunshine, so we can never ever be afraid.

Thank You, Father, for all who have been teachers here, all who have now gone out into the world who were taught here and live as Christians in their daily work and in their homes.

Thank You for those who teach us today, and love us and pray for us, that we too might live for Jesus.

Bless, O God, the parents of these children, give them patience in answering their questions, and joy in caring for them. Make their home a place where each lives for the other and all live for You.

Give us grace, we pray, to live at home with unselfishness and without moodiness when sometimes we are misunderstood - or think we are, for there is no place where we are known and loved more than in the family circle.

We pray, Father, for boys and girls in need:

> Those who will not have the opportunities that we have, of playing games or even walking, because of physical disability. Help them to use the gifts that they have that they may make their contribution to the human family.

> Those who live in bad housing conditions in our inner cities. Bless all boys and girls in need - the known and the unknown, and bless us too, Father, for Jesus' sake.

Amen

Church Anniversary

Almighty God, our heavenly Father, we praise and adore You that You established Your Church among men and commissioned her to preach the Gospel to every creature.

More especially, on this day we give thanks for everything that the Church has meant to us in the days that are past.

The times when we came here downcast and discouraged and went away with fresh life in us. Occasions when we came fighting a battle with the fascination of wrong things and found the grace to keep clean, and times when we came into the holy place with a sore heart and found Your comfort.

We give thanks for the truth of Your Word, O God, the preachers who interpret it, inspired by Your Holy Spirit.

The loyalty and dedication of Officers and Teachers here today, and the memory of all who were in the service of the Kingdom in days gone by and have joined the Church triumphant; for the means of grace and the hope of glory.

Forgive us that we have not always seen our responsibility, the dullness of our vision, our lack of imagination and understanding of Your truth.

Baptise us afresh with Your life-giving Spirit and send us out as ambassadors of Christ. Help us to proclaim boldly the Good News of the Gospel; give to us the prophets' scorn of tyranny, and a Christ-like tenderness for the weary and heavy laden. Show us how to seek the lost, and cease from seeking our own life, lest we lose it.

Bless all our work among young people, we pray, and all who labour in our community that lives may be helped and enriched.

Bless all who, this day are in need of Your help and healing. We commit ourselves anew to Your service, for we would be not only hearers of Your word, but doers also - so shall men know that we are disciples of Jesus.

Hear us for His sake. **Amen.**

World Church

Our Father God, we are thankful for our fellowship in the company of all faithful people throughout the world, and this day we are mindful of the world-wide Church.

Unite us in prayer and praise with Christians everywhere. Your love embraces us all, Your grace sufficient for every need, Your Holy Spirit boundless.

Bless us here and give to us the vision of a world where all the barriers that divide us are broken down, and love is all.

Forgive us, we pray, our wilful ignorance of Your work overseas, our lack of interest, our preoccupation with our place of worship here.

Grant that we may be baptised afresh into a sense of the needs of our fellows. Quicken our spirits, give to us a heart of compassion that Jesus knew.

Prompt us to sacrificial giving in gratitude for all that we possess, and help us to see in our contribution to the work, bodies healed, minds enlightened, souls saved, the hungry fed, and ignorance give place to knowledge, and men and women living to the full.

We pray, Father, for all who are working overseas, taking the Gospel of Your redeeming love that men and women may be whole - body, mind and spirit made new in Jesus.

We pray, for mission hospitals and schools. For the United Nations Organisation and all other agencies in this land and others who are seeking political solutions to the problems of disease, hunger and poverty.

We pray for Christians persecuted by the state or ostracised by their families - for all who have recently found new life in Christ, keep them faithful, Lord.

Accept, we pray, our thanks for all the privileges that we enjoy. Enlarge our vision, rekindle our zeal, and use us in Your service for Jesus' sake. Amen.

One World - His World

O God our Father, who sent Jesus, the Prince of Peace, that we, through Him might be reconciled to You, we thank You for His coming, His Kingdom is already here, in our hearts and in our attitude to all men everywhere.

We pray for Your world:
    For the differing nations who make their contribution to it.
    For their leaders and governments.
    For those who are struggling towards better living for their people.
    For Christians who serve the Third World.
    For refugees and relief agencies.

Strengthen, we pray, all who are working for true peace, justice and brotherhood among the nations.

Forgive us, Father:
    That the vision of one world has failed to find a place in our thinking.
    That we have grown insensitive to the poverty and suffering in other parts of the world - it doesn't hurt us any more. Your children, the world over are one in need, for our hearts are alike, despite our difference in colour and culture.

We are one in need of forgiveness and guidance.
We are one in need of food, clothing and adequate shelter.
We are one in need of land that will grow crops.
We are one in desiring to live and see our children grow up healthy and in freedom from fear.

Help us, Lord, with our expanding knowledge to use new forces aright - to save life and not destroy it.
Help Your church to continue her ministry of reconciliation and healing, through Jesus Christ in whose service we are.

                                                                            Amen.

The Family of Man

O God our Father, we come to You with glad hearts, a quiet serenity
about us, and with praise for Your redeeming grace.
We thank You for the life that is ours,
and our new life in Jesus –
our new sight, for we were blind and now we see,
for our new insight into Your ways with us;
and the new family to which we belong,
for You have enlarged our relationships, we belong to all men and
women - everywhere.
At the Cross our burdened hearts found release, our sins were
forgiven, our fears dissolved, our inner battles ceased.
But there are burdens, Lord, from which we do not want to be
released. The trials and tribulations of others have become more
really ours.
Who is weak and I am not weak?
Whose family have been bereaved and I am not bereaved?
Whose hopes have been disappointed and I am not disappointed?
Whose pain hurts and I am not hurt?
We pray, with feeling, our Saviour Christ for:
Those who are suffering because of oppressive governments
throughout the world. Those, who through no fault of their own
suffer - one parent families, victims of crime and road accidents,
those born with disabilities, and all who have to live with a sense
of shame because of what a member of the family has done.
Forgive us that the news of tragedy on our television screen does not
hurt us as it ought. We know that we cannot bear all the world's
sufferings upon our hearts, but we can pray for them, and we do so
now.
Give to us a deeper concern for world peace, a more enlightened
understanding of world problems.
Help us to take our stand with those who campaign for disarmament,
and all who seek a more just and equitable world.
Hear our prayer in the Name of Jesus and for His sake.
Amen.

Harvest Thanksgiving

We thank You, Father, for this world in which we live - Your world.
For the seasons with their peculiar charm –
> the Spring with its new life, reminding us of our new life in Jesus, and our need of constant renewal.
> For summertime, the miracle of flowers and summer fruits; You do more than supply our need, You give us things to delight us.
> And we are in autumn, the season of the yellowing leaf and the ripened harvest, tasks brought to fulfilment, food for the cattle, and for ourselves.

Thank You, Father, for autumn and all its loveliness, may we grow lovely growing older.

Give us hearts to see all lovely things, for often, our sin, our petulant moods, our selfishness, blind us to the beauty of nature. One sin can spoil the loveliest of days, as it can spoil our life.
> And our clean heart can give to a dandelion a loveliness that only a pure heart can give it.

Bless, O God, all countrymen, Farmer, Stockman, Labourer, Shepherd, and their families - and rural communities, Church and Chapel, Women's Institutes and Young Farmers' Clubs.

But we pray too, Father, for all who contribute to our standard of living; throughout the world harvests ripen, in tea plantation and fruit farm, and there are those who bring to us the silver harvest of the sea.

Forgive us that so often our food is taken with little thanks, and remind us that there is famine in many lands, and our fellows die for lack of food and water. Give us a deeper understanding of their needs, and compassion in our hearts for the poor and needy.

Bless, we pray, all who are working in Christian Aid, Cafod, Tear Fund, Oxfam, and organisations seeking to meet human need;

Bless Your Church with a larger vision, a deeper commitment in service and the zeal of a Spirit-filled life.

Amen.

Women's Fellowship/Young Wives

O God, our Father, we come with gratitude in our hearts for the life that is ours, You love us, we are loved within the Fellowship of Your people, we are loved in our Families. For all that we know of love, we bless Your Holy Name.

Forgive us, that there has often been little of love within us, our attitudes prejudiced, we have done our duty, but refused the second mile.

We have done the right thing, but with little grace, been kind, but our kindness has not been from an overflowing heart - it hasn't cost us very much.

O unexampled Love, help us to love with the Spirit of Jesus, and in all our giving, give our self - heart and mind, as He did.

We give thanks for all that women have contributed through the ages, to our living today, for the saints and martyrs and the pioneers of yesterday, and for the many today, within the Church - and outside it, who are in the service of their fellows.

Bless, we pray, Women's Fellowships everywhere, and Young Wives groups - bless the work amongst women in this church and area.

Bless wives and mothers in the fellowship of home, we recall the guiding influence of our own parents, and thank You for all that they were, and all that they taught us - the sacrifices they made for us, and their belief in us.

Bless, Father, homes that this day need Your help, comfort the bereaved, guide the perplexed, befriend the lonely - lead us into situations where we can bring Your love to a needy soul.

Bless our home with Your peace and love that we may be able to serve others for Jesus' sake.

Amen.

Remembrance Sunday

Eternal God, our heavenly Father, You have made of one blood all the nations of men, we pray for ourselves and all men everywhere.
We belong together, in one world - Your world.
You have provided for our every need that we may live adequately from adequate resources, yet we have spoiled it all through our wilful disobedience to Your will.
The fruits of the earth can feed us all, yet Your children starve for want of food, for nations, like people, can be selfish. We have substituted patriotism for Your Kingdom of love, so nations live for themselves - their own interests, but we are one world. We are one in need of Your correction, too, and in need of forgiveness. Forgive us, O Lord.
We have used new knowledge to destructive ends, for nation cannot trust nation. Forgive us, O God.
Turn the leaders of the nations to the knowledge of Your truth through Jesus Christ, who lives and reigns on the throne of the universe - a throne that has never been empty.
O Blessed God, in whose hands are the keeping of the souls of men, we remember before You, all who have died in war, especially any dear to us, grant, that at the last, they, with us, may be presented faultless before the presence of Your glory with exceeding joy.
We pray for:
All who suffer and bear, bravely, the afflictions of war. Mothers, wives and children, bereft of loved ones. Deepen our understanding of their needs, and help us to bear one another's burdens and so fulfil the law of Christ.

Let us pray for peace.
O God, our Father, whose Blessed Son is the Prince of Peace, we pray for all leaders of nations that they may learn Your will and pursue policies that will lead to a better understanding among the world family.
We pray for all who are engaged in peace movements throughout the world; for men and women and young people are tired of a world

of mistrust and suspicion - the spirit of peace is moving in the hearts and minds of men - a new vision of a sharing, caring world. Bless all who are seeking peace.

We pray, Father, that we ourselves may be peaceable in all our relationships, free of prejudice, counting all men equal to us, in Jesus there is no East or West, all are one in Him.

Renew our faith in Your unchanging purpose of goodwill and peace upon earth, for the sake of Jesus Christ, who came to reconcile us to You, and ourselves to our fellows.

Amen.

Families, Friends and especially the Elderly

Most Blessed God, You have called us into the Kingdom of Your
dear Son, provided for our every need,
been to us, in times of trial, our strength;
in times of perplexity, the answer to our problem,
we bless You for all the good we receive at Your hand.
Lead us, by Your Holy Spirit to things eternal.
We join with the whole company of Your people, in heaven and on
earth, in rejoicing in Your unchanging love.
You have given to us, kindred and friends, and there are times when
we are unworthy of them.
Letters are unwritten, and kindnesses not done – we will do it
tomorrow – it's always 'tomorrow', Lord, tomorrow. Forgive us.
Good intentions are ours, but they never seem to get beyond the
intent. Forgive us.
We are less generous than we think we are – help us to know that we
are stewards of all we possess.
Make us generous in our thoughts of others, quick to praise and slow
to condemn – to speak the word of encouragement more freely,
and to criticise less.
We thank You, O God, for family and friends.
We pray for:
Families separated because a member is in hospital – especially for
the elderly in Geriatric wards. Those who nurse them there – and
at home, often alone, but devotedly.
For Help the Aged, Methodist Homes and all who care for those in
the autumn-tide of life working for their welfare.
Bless all wardens in sheltered accommodation, especially those in our
community.
Give to us a deeper understanding of the needs of frail people when
they visit us in our homes – help us to be imaginative and to
anticipate things that will make for their comfort.
And bind us all together in the family of Your Fatherhood, through
Jesus Christ, who shared at Nazareth the life of the family.   Amen.

Bible Sunday/Christian Communications

We give thanks, O God our Father, for the life that is ours in Jesus Christ Your Son, our Saviour.

In every age You have spoken with men, but supremely You have spoken with us in the Word made flesh - Jesus, who, through the eyes of faith, we have seen and heard for ourselves.

When we were dead to the truth about ourselves, dead to every noble aspiration, You made us alive in Him. For this we praise You.

We thank You that in the scriptures we see Your way of dealing with us - never according to our sins, but always by Your mercy and grace; that in times of stress we have the comfortable words of Jesus, and when we are in danger of losing our way - falling to temptation, You have provided a way of escape, and we stand firm on the promises He made to us.

We pray for all who seek to interpret Your Word for us - theologians, commentators and preachers. For the Bible Societies and those whose task is its translation into other languages.

We thank You for those who have the gift of creative writing, weaving words for the illumination of our minds and the uplift of our spirits.

Bless, Lord, all Christian publishers, religious newspaper and magazine editors.

Give to us a deeper concern for the written word, for there is literature that lies unread, and we deprive ourselves of much truth and beauty in poetry and books that could inspire us. May Your Holy Spirit give to us that sensitivity of heart, deepening our insight, inspiring and teaching us that we may live more fully, through Jesus Christ, our Lord.

Amen.

Family Service

Let us thank God for all His goodness.
Thank You, Father God.
For the wonderful world in which we live.
Thank You, Father God.
For the companionship of home and friends.
Thank You, Father God.
For healthy limbs and active minds.
Thank You, Father God.
For laughter and fun.
Thank You, Father God.
For those who love us, though we are not always loveable.
Thank You, Father God.

Let us ask His forgiveness for the unlovely things in our lives;
We are sorry
    For being sulky when we do not get our own way.
    For being selfish.
    For unkind thoughts toward others.
    For being disobedient to our parents or teachers.
Lord Jesus Christ, forgive us. Make us like Yourself, generous,
    loving, obedient and kind.

Let us remember boys and girls who do not have our advantages;
    Those who are disabled and find it hard to walk and play games.
    Those without good homes in our towns and cities.
    Those who are living in refugee camps throughout the world.
    All who hunger - for food, education and a better way of life.

Lord, hear our prayer.
And in Your mercy, answer their needs and call us to serve them in love, for Your sake, for You said; *"As we do it to them, we do it to You"*.

                                                          Amen

Evening Prayer

O Blessed God, in whom is light and no darkness at all, as the evening shadows fall and the night comes, lead us again into the light of Your love. May there be in this hour a clearer light to shine upon the road that leads to Jesus.

We ask forgiveness for the things that this past week we have left undone, and the things we have never even attempted; for the things that we have left half finished, and the things we have put off until tomorrow. We have so many good intentions Lord. Forgive us for our wasted time and lost opportunities.
Forgive us, O God.

We thank You for today, and for any new truth that we have learned from Your Word, for the time we have spent with those whom we love, for the desire to worship here in this place, and the grace which is sufficient for our every need.

Bless, we pray, this night, those who will be working while we sleep, doctors and nurses and all whose task tonight will be to ease pain; to bring a new life into the world, or to close the eyes of those for whom this life is ending.

Bless those in industry who must work through the night to help us live tomorrow - those who produce newspapers, those who bring our letters.

Bless parents who will be awake with little children who cannot sleep. Be near those in pain, comfort the sorrowing, bless each one of us and help us to witness with courage, to walk in purity and to serve with love.

Give to us Yourself, O God, then we shall be able for all things.

Hear our prayer in the name of Jesus, and for His blessed sake.
Amen.

Citizens of Two Worlds

Almighty God, most merciful Father, Creator of all that is - yet near to every loving heart in the life and teaching of Jesus, in the quietness help us to worship with reality.

We come as citizens of heaven, yet we belong to this community - this land, this world. Bless this land of ours that it may be a blessing to the world.

Grant that our ideals and aspirations may be in accord with Your will. Keep us from hypocrisy in feeling and action. Grant us sound government and just laws, good education and a clean press; simplicity and justice in all our relations with one another, and above all, a spirit of service which will abolish pride of place and inequality of opportunity.

O God, our Father, give wisdom, courage and uprightness to all who are in places of authority. Keep them loyal to Christian ideals and unwearied in service.

We pray for all who are in local government, especially in our own area. Continue to raise up men and women who offer themselves as servants of the community as a vocation to You.

Help us always to know that we are members one of another, that if someone in this place where we live suffers, we also suffer, for they are part of this family.

So, we pray for those in pain, the sad, the bereaved, those who draw near to the close of their earthly life, for those passing through anxiety, those whose hearts are bitter, and for all who have secret trials and for whom the help of others is vain.

Fill our hearts with deep compassion for these our fellows, and hasten the day when Your Kingdom of justice and truth shall dawn, and the earth be filled with the knowledge of Your love, and the peace that passes understanding reign in the hearts of all.

Hear us for Jesus Christ's sake.

Amen.

Having Courage

Most gracious God, full of compassion and tender mercy, we come to You in our weakness, make us strong.
We come in need of forgiveness, forgive us, we pray - forgive us all that spoils us.
We come needing light on our perplexities, give us eyes to see what we ought to do.
We come with our fears, dissolve them in Your love. We need healing, O Great Physician of our souls, make us whole again through Jesus Christ, Your Son, our Lord.

We thank You for Jesus; His courage in His ministry. His courage when opposition was strong. His courage in the Temple court. His courage in the garden of Gethsemane, and before Pilate; His courage on the Cross.

Give us courage too, Lord. The courage of our feelings. The courage of our convictions. The courage to be in a minority of one. Give us courage when adversity comes to us, courage in the crisis, courage to bear pain, and courage to begin again when some venture has failed. Give us courage to try new ways in the work which is dear to our heart. Give us courage, Lord.

We give thanks for the pioneers of yesterday who were bold in fighting injustices in society, those who were not disobedient to the heavenly vision; and for our fathers in the faith who were persecuted for their belief and have left us a glorious heritage.

O Holy Spirit of God, quicken our imagination, open our minds to opportunities, and give us the power to use them. Make us gentle in dealing with others' trials, and give us patience in our own. Help us to serve, in newness of life, and with tenderness, the sick, the sad, and the sinful, in the name of Jesus, who came not to be ministered to but to minister and give Himself for our redemption.
Amen.

Things Unseen

O God, our Father, we thank You for the enrichment of our life in fellowship with You. You have set eternity in our hearts and planted Your image within us.

We mourn our concern for transient things, the trifles of the passing hour that so often distract our minds from high endeavours and set our thoughts upon unworthy ends; yet we are thankful that nothing temporal has power to satisfy our souls.

We spend our days among the mortal and the seen, and because the world is so much with us, and we have responsibilities to meet the material needs of ourselves and our family, we have little sight for unseen things, and we have missed You at every turn. Every common bush may flame with fire, but we have no time to look, nor eyes of insight to comprehend the holy ground.

Forgive us, Father, for there is a longing within for more than bread. We need Jesus, the Bread of Life - we need to become as little children again, to live in a wonderful world as He did - the Father's world, where the wonder and bloom of the world about us can gladden our hearts and give us eternal values.

Give to us the childlike heart that every day may be a glorious adventure. Pierce the earthborn clouds that hide the loveliness from us - the mists of prejudice, anxiety and unbelief; the mood of self-pity.

Help us to know, that however dark the night the morning always comes, spring always follows winter and that all things work together for good to those who love You. For that has been our experience again and again.

Hear us, Lord, for others. For those who cannot see other than themselves or their own family. Those who are insensitive to loveliness - in nature - in little children - in fine deeds.

O Saviour Christ, who brought new light into darkened eyes, and a new tenderness to stay the tears of men, hear our prayer and daily give us eyes to see others' needs, for still You love and care, for all men everywhere.

Amen.

Bearing Others' Burdens

O God our Father, we come to You with glad hearts, a quiet serenity about us, and with praise for Your redeeming grace. We thank You for the life that is ours, and our new life in Jesus - our new sight, for we were blind and now we see, for our new insight into Your ways with us; and the new family to which we belong, for You have enlarged our relationships, we belong to all men and women - everywhere.

At the Cross our burdened hearts found release, our sins were forgiven, our fears, dissolved, our inner battles ceased. But there are burdens, Lord, from which we do not want to be released. The trials and tribulations of others have become more really ours.

Who is weak and I am not weak? Whose family have been bereaved and I am not bereaved? Whose hopes have been disappointed and I am not disappointed? Whose pain hurts and I am not hurt?

We pray, with feeling, our Saviour Christ for;

Those who are suffering because of oppressive governments throughout the world. Those, who through no fault of their own suffer - one parent families, victims of crime and road accidents, those born handicapped, and all who have to live with a sense of shame because of what a member of the family has done.

Forgive us that the news of tragedy on our television screen does not hurt us as it ought. We know that we cannot bear all the world's sufferings upon our hearts, but we can pray for them, and we do so, now.

Give to us a deeper concern for world peace, a more enlightened understanding of world problems. Help us to take our stand with those who campaign for Peace and Justice, and all who seek a more just and equitable world. Hear our prayer in the Name of Jesus and for His sake.

Amen.

May Our Faith Be Deepened

Grant O God, that in this hour of worship our faith may be deepened, our understanding enlightened, our wills surrendered to Your will, and Your peace possess our souls.

We give thanks for all the mercies we have received at Your hand; for the bounty that has sustained us and the discipline that has corrected us, and for Your infinite patience with us.

We do not forget, O God, that we have never perfectly loved You, unworthy thoughts have come between us and Your self, fear has taken away our freedom, and in anxiety we have lost our trusting.

Forgive us Father, and help us again to know that simple faith that was ours when we first believed.

We have been very busy Lord, with so many very necessary things, our daily tasks, meeting the needs of a family, earning a living, but we have not always done it with grace.
Show us how to live with serenity of heart.

When moments of decision are with us, help us to choose aright, when emergencies are upon us, help us to be calm;
when duty calls, may we do it with Your Spirit.

But not for ourselves only would we pray, O God,
we pray for others too:
For all who are in danger by land, sea and air.
The sick and suffering.
The bereaved and sorrowful.
For those who wish they were dead.
For those battling with some secret sin.
For those whose marriage is breaking up.

We pray for all in need, and remind ourselves that we also need Your grace day by day.

So, help us Lord, for Jesus Christ's sake.

Amen

Guidance

Our Father God, from the confusion of voices in the world, we come into the inner world in this moment.

Speak with us. We come in the name of Jesus, who spoke - and still speaks, gracious words of comfort or challenge, encouragement or kindly reproof for our soul's health. We would hear Him. May every voice be stilled save His voice. Give us ears to hear, and hearts to understand the truth about ourselves and the truth of Your word.

We give thanks for those who influenced our lives for good and gave to us the Good News of the Gospel.

As we look back upon our life it seems that we had to meet certain people, that our steps have been guided, that You had a plan and purpose for us. Help us always to know Your will and to do it, so shall we be led aright. We are not wise enough to know the way we ought to take, but guided by Your Holy Spirit, we shall not stray into dead-ends that lead to nowhere.

We thank You for the guidance we receive in Your Word - in the teaching of Jesus; for guidance through our enlightened conscience, and guidance through the inner voice - Your Spirit meeting with our spirit. Our Christian experience has given us a concern for others, our eyes have been opened to anticipate needs; help us to act in that moment when we have 'a concern' for someone, to do the Christlike thing, so, may someone's prayer be answered.

We confess, with shame, the good intentions of our heart that we have failed to carry out - because it was too costly, or because we feared that our action might have been taken the wrong way. Help us to act upon our Christlike compulsions while the heart is warm, for tomorrow may be too late.

Use us, Lord, as instruments of Your purposes as You used others in bringing us to discipleship. Where You lead we will follow.

Hear us for Your name's sake. **Amen.**

Living In Love
(1 Corinthians 13)

O God our Father, whose nature and name is love - love beyond our deserving, unmerited and free, help us to know what true love is, and to live it.

Love is kind, so help us to be kind - thoughtful in the little things that mean so much; The uncalled for act of generosity to someone. The remembrance of an anniversary date, of gladness or sadness. The letter of congratulation - or condolence. Help us to be kind.

And patient - patient with those who tell us an oft-repeated tale. Enable us to hear it again, with grace. Give us patience when we lose heart because the coming of Your Kingdom seems so slow to come. Give us the quiet spirit in a bustling, impatient world.

And if love is not jealous, Lord, help us to know that all things are ours - penniless we own the world. How can we ever be jealous when our hearts are filled with Your Spirit.

Nor can we ever be boastful, we have nothing that we have not received at Your hands and the hand of others. Keep us humble, Lord, not thinking of ourselves more highly than we ought to think. Keep us aware of our creatureliness, yet holding our heads high, for we are Your children.

Make us glad in others' successes, for we know that it is often easier to weep with those who weep than to rejoice with those who rejoice.

Help us to love, Lord Jesus, with all that we have and all that we are, for Your sake.

Amen.

We Deserve Nothing

Eternal and ever loving Father, we give thanks for all that we receive from Your bounteous hand - gifts that sustain our lives, day by day to keep us healthy and alive.

We thank You for reason and conscience, for nurture and guidance - for all the gifts of nature and of grace.

We praise You, we bless You, we worship You for all Your goodness towards us, Your unworthy children.

We are conscious that we deserve nothing, but Your nature is always to give, and You do - accept the gratitude of our hearts.

Give to us, we pray, the trusting heart of childhood, for we recall that we never doubted that our needs would be met, never worried about tomorrow. We were loved and cared for.

Give us the simplicity that was once ours. We were without guile, truthful and candid. But now our living seems often tangled and complicated. The world has done something to us. Help us to know that simplicity that was in Jesus, that every day may be an adventure in living in an exciting world.

Help us to live the guided life, obeying the leading of the inner-voice which is the prompting of Your Holy Spirit - to do the Christlike thing, not asking to know where it will lead, but content to obey.

Forgive us, O God that we have often been deaf to Your voice, or pretended that we were, and so have missed opportunities of doing good. For all our failures in love, we ask forgiveness.

Help us to witness to the new life that is ours in Jesus Christ, by word and action, kindness and generosity, honesty in all our dealings, straightforward in speech, magnanimous in our judgements and sensitive to need.

Bless all who are in need today, and all who seek to care for them.

We dedicate ourselves again, Lord, to our high calling.

Hear us for Jesus Christ's sake.

Amen.

King of Kings

O God, our Father, we thank You for Jesus Christ, the Light of the world, and our Saviour from sin, our helper in every time of trouble, our strength in weakness, our refuge in times of temptation.

We thank You for Jesus - that in Him we see Your mind and love. We praise You that He poured out His soul to death for us and for our salvation. We thank You for His Kingship over the whole of history - and His Kingship in our lives. But we confess with shame that we have not always obeyed Him.

Forgive us our disloyalties, our deceptions, our insincerities. Forgive us for being careless about the feelings of others and sensitive about our own - demanding standards from others which we seldom fulfil ourselves.

Forgive us, O God. And equip us to meet the tasks and problems of this life, courage to take the right decision when it is hard to take, endurance to keep steadily on when we would rather give up, patience to bear with people even when they are foolish and misguided, and sympathy to try to understand rather than to condemn.

Bless, Father, those for whom life has become wearisome - one grey task after another in lonely days.

Bless those who are so tired and overworked that they become difficult to live with.

Bless Your Church throughout the world, and so cleanse, purify and strengthen her that we may be used in the service of the Kingdom. Remind us that wherever we are there is the Church. We pray for all our officers in this place - all who teach - and preach. Bless our minister, Lord, and his family.

Bless all whom we love - those away from us, and those near, keep us - and them, in Your fear and favour, until the long day closes and we reach our home at length, our task here ended and life anew begun.

Hear us, in the Saviour's name, and for His blessed sake,

Amen

Today While It Is Here

O God our Father, giver of every good and perfect gift, we bless You for the supreme gift of Yourself in Jesus - the Word made flesh that men could see, and know Your love for them, in Him.

We thank You for His ministry, His healing, and teaching, the serenity of His unhurried life in His ever-filled days, and for His moment by moment trust and implicit obedience to Your will.

Give to us, we pray, a like trust and obedience day by day. We do not ask to see tomorrow, but just to live fully today. Help us to know the complete joy of a surrendered life and a peace within that no outward circumstance can shatter.

Help us, today, to grasp our opportunities - To be kind by listening to another when they want to unburden themselves.
To be unselfish with our time when we could plead that we are so busy.
To anticipate a need and to act before we are asked.
To surprise someone with practical love.
And help us, in this faith of ours, not to hug it too closely to our breast.

Give us the ability to feel for others:-
For the shy.
For the mother whose boy is not as other boys are.
For the woman separated from her husband, the man who has lost his wife, through no fault of his own, but another's sin.
We pray for the teenager who finds school life hard and young people for whom society can find no work.

By Your grace, Lord, may we never seek to wound them by the careless words that often come unthinkingly from our lips. Show us how we may answer their need without being condescending.

Use us today, Father, that our neighbourhood may be better for our living.

Hear us for Jesus' sake.

Amen.

Make Us Less Selfish

O Eternal God, whom to know is life indeed, and whom to serve is the fulfilment of our lives, we praise You that through Jesus Christ we have access to You; that through Him, we know that Your nature and Your name is love, and we can call You Father.

So, we come into the family fellowship from our wanderings of the past week.

We are more than a little tired of the alien atmosphere in which we live where the world family is broken by divisions of race and class, and where hearts are broken by war and men, women and children die for lack of food. And we are conscious of our own inadequacy, our sins of the spirit to which we, as Christians, are prone.

Forgive us, Father, that we may begin again, our hearts cleansed, our vision widened, our minds enlightened, our faith strengthened and our serving more meaningful from this hour, for Jesus Christ's sake.

Save us, O God, from the spirit that knows everything, for there is much that we do not know.

May we never make another feel small or insignificant in our company by parading the little knowledge that is ours. Give to us the simplicity that was in Jesus who was at one with all men from all walks of life.

Make us less selfish, for often self is at the centre of our living - we are touchy, easily hurt when no one notices the good that we do.

Give to us the magnanimous spirit that was in Jesus, who, when He was reviled, did not answer.

We thank You for all our blessings - the love we share, at home, friendship, and the loyalty of kindred spirits.

Bless all who this day are in need, especially those homes saddened by the loss of loved ones. We pray for Your Church in divided communities, such as Northern Ireland, seeking to reconcile differing factions.

And bless us too, Father, keep us near the Cross in all our living this week for Jesus' sake.

Amen

Inner Freedom

O God our Father, we thank You for all Your mercies - Your goodness that sustains us, Your Fatherly discipline that corrects us, Your love that redeems us.

We acknowledge, Father, our weak faith, our slowness of heart to believe the promises of Jesus and to commit ourselves to Him.

Forgive us our pride and self-sufficiency, our foolish efforts to live by our own power and wisdom. Help us continue to know that trust that was ours when we first came into Your Kingdom, and enable us to draw continually upon divine resources.

We pray for all prisoners; For the prisoners of conscience in countries throughout the world.
The prisoners whom society has shut away because of conduct that society cannot condone - we pray for them, and their families.
The prisoners condemned to live in atrocious conditions in the 'twilight zones' of our towns and cities.
The prisoners who are shackled by a physical handicap or abnormality.
The prisoners whose guilty conscience will not let them rest.

We remind ourselves that Jesus came to set the prisoner free - enable those of our fellows who are shut in to hear that knock on the door of their inmost being, and in responding, know that inner freedom that circumstances cannot shackle.

Bless, we pray, all who are seeking to reclaim and rehabilitate the prisoners, who, by their words, and by their lives proclaim the Gospel of Jesus.

Hear us in the name of Jesus in whom we are free indeed.

Amen.

Life's Gladness

We thank You, Father for the way in which You show Your love for us in the everyday world of our life.

We have known days of routine drabness - then You surprise us with the surprise of joy, and we are lifted out of our wretched mood and life takes on a new meaning.
Someone calls whom we had not expected, and it makes our day. Someone is full of gratitude for something we had done, and we had forgotten all about it, we are simply glad that You used us in service.
Someone says, "I love You". A little child smiles on seeing us and clings to us. Someone makes us feel wanted by asking our help.

We thank You for the ministry of surprise; for those little things that happen so unexpectedly because there is grace in another's heart and they have translated it into love by their kindness.

Give to us, we pray, the Spirit of Jesus who made love a real thing - something to be shared, something to be glad about in the commonplace of every day living.

Take from our hearts the stress of living in busy, noisy cities with screaming planes overhead and everyone in a hurry below, and help us to live with the beauty of Your peace within when all seems confusion without.

May we never be too busy to be kind. Give to us the serenity of an ordered life, and may someone be glad that they met us on the road today.

Forgive us, O God, if our eyes have been blind to the needs of our fellows - blind to the loveliness of Your world, blind because of a stubborn will, we did not want to see for it might involve us in something uncongenial to us.

Bless all who this day have known gladness, may they find in their joy the Giver of every good and perfect gift and give to us all joy in believing.

Amen.

The Flickering Flame

O God our Father, whose loving kindness is over all our days, we give thanks for Your goodness at all times and in every place. You have shielded and rescued us, helped and guided us.

We thank You for all that has made the unseen real to us, and for every experience that has taught us, in a changing world to cling more closely to Your unchanging grace.

But we confess, Father, that the drift of earthly thought has come between our souls and You; even in our highest moments there has been something of self.

Forgive us, renew us by Your Holy Spirit, give us a deeper faith, grant us courage and insight to more effectively serve the present age.

Your Blessed Son called His disciples to shine as lights in a dark world, and our light has been flickering for some time now for it is not always seen by the world that we possess a power for life; there has been little to distinguish our living from the lives of others, we have done no more than they do. Nor have we been as sacrificial as some are in noble causes.

Give us O God, again, that passion that once we knew for holiness and service, for men and women are in the darkness, frustrated and afraid, sick of the sins that they haven't the power to break.

Jesus has shown us how to live gloriously, help us to believe that what He has done for us He can do for others also.

Fill us with the Spirit, Lord, that we may evangelise. We are not all called to 'go into all the world and preach the Gospel', but we can go into our world tomorrow - our street, our community, our workplace witnessing with our life, and speaking, as we are led to do so, some word of comfort or challenge for Christ's sake.

Sanctify our imaginations, Lord Jesus, guide us to those who are in need and bless our endeavours,

for Your name's sake. **Amen.**

In The Quietness

Let us spend a moment in silence.

Help us, in the quietness of this place, to hear Your voice O God.
   Take from our souls the strain and stress of the past week.
   We praise You for Your blessed love, and for Your faithfulness, despite our sinning, Your goodness despite our unworthiness, and Your comfort when we need it most.
   Your grace is sufficient for all our needs.
   Help us to rest our lives in You.

We thank You, Father, for the life that is ours - for the joy of waking up to exciting days where anything may happen in Your world. Thanks for the glad surprises of life - for friends whom sometimes we don't deserve, for we neglect them. Thanks for the opportunities that come to us, of doing good to another, help us always to do it with stealth.

We thank You for words of encouragement when we have failed in a task, for there are those who will still believe in us, and enable us to carry on.

Give us grace, O God, to do those things that we find it hard to do - help us to treat with love, the people whom we do not like, remembering that we too have our failings and faults.
   Make us honest and humble enough to admit when we are wrong and not try to save face.

Take from us all resentments - against life, and people, especially those whose opinions and attitudes to life differ widely from ours.

Hear us, Father, as we bring to You, in faith and love, our prayers for those who are in need of mercy and comfort - those, for whom the light has gone out in bereavement, those who know no peace and comfort at home, for they have wretched accommodation, those torn with inner conflicts and those whose conscience will not let them rest.

Wherever there is need, Lord, help us meet it, in the name of Jesus.
   Hear our prayer in His name. **Amen.**

Every Day A Holy Day

We thank You, Father, for the first day of the week, this day of resurrection - and for this place, the community of Your people. We may know You everywhere, but coming together for worship, has, for men and women through the ages, had special meaning.

Here, we shake off the dust of our travelling, and are made clean again - our sins forgiven, as we confess them now.

Thank You, Father, for forgiveness.

We give thanks for the joy of living, a life to lead, a path to tread and a journey that excites us as each day dawns and we venture forth with You.

Help us to use each day well, others will share the day with us - those with whom we work, those whom we meet in brief encounters on the road, help us to live as those who know the secret of abundant living.

And, as Your Holy Spirit guides us, enable us to know the moment when we ought to speak the word of challenge, and when to keep silent, when to speak words of comfort and when to warn, and to do it all in the Spirit of Jesus.

Bless, O God, those who have taken the wrong way, open their eyes to their own foolishness, and call them back before they bring shame to themselves and sorrow to others.

Bless those who have made mistakes, give them humility to confess their errors, and courage to start again.

Speak, we pray, to those who will listen to no warning, and will accept no advice, save them, Lord, from their own folly. And live within us, O Holy Spirit of God, that people may know where to go when help is needed, and to whom they can turn for a shoulder to cry on; then, by Your grace, may they know Your help and healing.

Hear us, for Your Love's sake. **Amen.**

We Can Win Through

Eternal and most merciful Father, we praise You for all the gifts that You have given to us, the truth that You have shown to us, and for the love which constantly surrounds us.

We thank You for Your saving grace in Jesus Christ and for every spiritual blessing that is ours in Him - forgiveness, peace of heart and mind, and joy that no one, or any thing can ever take away from us.

We thank You for His comfort in our sorrow, His strength in our weakness and His guidance in our perplexity.

There is gratitude in our hearts, Father, for this pilgrimage of life - this journey through the different-patterned days.
We have known joy, and the sunshine of Your love which has given us a light heart.
We have known peace in many a blessed moment - when we have been with those whom we love, when we have shared the silence with a well-loved friend.
We have known grief, times when our hearts have been bewildered and painful, and we have known You there.

Remind us, Father, when despair is very real and we are at our wits-end, that there were others who knew it also, those who wrestled hard with doubts and fears and won through.

Remind us that we are surrounded by a great cloud of witnesses, and may our remembrance of them give us new courage.

We pray for those who suffer, Lord, especially any known to us.
For those who are on the point of giving up.
For those who nurse some secret fear that they have never shared with anyone - help them to share it with You.

We pray for the successful, keep them humble, and for the failures, help them to a new beginning.

And enable us for all that life will demand of us this week.

Amen.

Belonging Together

O Blessed God whose light is truth and whose warmth is love, we come to You for light for our pathway and the warmth of Your companionship in Jesus. In fellowship with Him we are truly human for His grace is the source of all human loveliness.

Touch our hearts, Lord, make firm our wills, then in utter dependence upon You, send us out to live the faith that we believe.

We thank You for fellowship, the fellowship of kindred hearts and minds. You did not create us to live solitary lives, but have given to us others whom we love and care for. Help us always to treat men and women as sacred personalities, and in an age when people tend to be manipulated for other ends, may we never seek to take advantage of them for selfish gain.

Forgive us, Father, when we tend to see only the faults of others and never the good in them. Forgive us when we put a stumbling block in another's way by some unconscious action of ours - or some word thoughtlessly spoken, or by our attitude to life.

Help us to believe in folk, even when they let us down, for we are mindful of the fact that someone believed in us - and still does believe, so shall the best be brought out in them.

And give us a concern for those in need – the hungry in need of bread, the sick in need of health, the guilty in need of forgiveness, the lonely in need of friendship, the young in search of a leader, and the old in need of assurance of the life to come.

We pray for those whose task is in dealing with human problems:- the probation officer, the welfare worker, the marriage-guidance counsellor, the shop-steward, the doctor, the minister, the chaplain.

Give us love, Lord towards our fellows everywhere for Your name's sake.

Amen.

Mission and Evangelism

We praise You, O God, we acknowledge You to be the Lord.

Assembled in the name of Jesus, we already know His presence with us. Bless us in this hour for Your name's sake.

Let us give thanks to God
 for the Gospel of redeeming love,
 for the power of Christ to meet the varying needs of men.
 For the miracle of conversion.
 For the opportunities of evangelism given to the Church.

Let us acknowledge with shame:
 Our complacency in a world of sin and our hesitating witness for Christ.
 Our reluctance to accept the cost of evangelism,
 our failure in love.
 Our lack of faith and prayer by which alone revival can come to our land.

O Blessed God, whom to know is life eternal, grant that each of us may become an ambassador of the Good News in our working life - at the office and in the factory and workshop, in the neighbourhood where we live.
 And give to us an insight into the spiritual needs of those with whom we are in daily contact.
 Deliver us from self-consciousness in speaking of our experience of Christ's love in our life.

We remember before You, Father, all who are chaplains in industry, colleges, universities and prisons. All who are engaged in the work of evangelism and all who are seeking the lost for Your sake - and theirs.

Renew in us the spirit of faith and service that men and women may find in Jesus the fulfilment of their lives.

Hear us for Jesus' sake. **Amen.**

The Restless Spirit

Let us spend a moment in silence

Jesus said; "Come to Me, all who labour and are heavy laden, and I will give you rest."

So, we come, Lord Jesus, for we have been restless, so many things have filled our moments and our days - very necessary things, our task at work, the needs and demands of the family, concern for a loved one, the problems that face us, the decisions we have to make.

Here in the quietness, help us to cast all our care upon You, for You care for us. You called Your disciples friends, we have a Friend in You - and You have a friend in us, so help us to trust You with our lives, to trust as we trust a best friend.
But we do not want this friendship to be one-sided, Lord, real friendship never is, so speak with us about the problems that You have with Your children - their selfishness in a world of hunger, their prejudices, of class or race, their unconcern for the under-privileged, their refusal of new ideas.

Have You spoken with us, Lord?

Forgive us that we ourselves have lived in a narrow world, widen our sympathies, quicken our imaginations, empower our will, and help us, by Your grace to know the thankful heart for all our blessings.

We have never known homelessness - nor starvation, our children are being educated, our doctor is readily available when we are ill, we have enough money to live comfortably, we enjoy our leisure time and the culture of the arts, millions of our fellows know none of these things.
Deepen our understanding of their needs, Lord Jesus, and show us how we can serve them, for Your name's sake.

Amen.

Life For All

O Blessed God, You call us to seek Your face, and so we come - to whom else can we go?
> You created us for Yourself, and in our inner beings we know it. You created us that we might live life to the full, and in Jesus You opened up the way to eternal life for all people everywhere.

We give thanks for the way in which You deal with Your wayward children – always with mercy and compassion, for we confess that we are unworthy of Your love.

We have not lived the faith that we profess.
> We have been fearful when we ought to have had trust in the promises of our Lord, been disobedient to the heavenly vision, and failed to venture when Your Holy Spirit called us to act.
> Nor have we yet learned the lesson of Calvary, for even in our best moments self has been there. Forgive us, Father for Jesus' sake.

We rejoice, O God, in the fellowship that we find in the company of Your people - those who bear one another's burdens, and share one another's joys; and for the mystical communion we have with those who have fought the good fight, finished the course, and kept the faith.

We give thanks for the gift of memory, so that those who are absent from us can be with us in spirit, and in a wonderful way, they still influence our lives.

Help us always to glory in our heritage in the Gospel, to fight against the injustices of the world as did the saints and pioneers of yesterday, empowered by Your Holy Spirit.

Hear us, Lord, for those in need. For those struggling against oppressive Governments.
> For the unemployed who are becoming bitter and frustrated, feeling that society has no use for them.
> For young people - missing from home, wandering abroad in our big cities.
> For those who are at the end of their tether and wish they were dead.

Lord, in Your mercy, hear us. **Amen.**

Holy Ground

Thank You, Father, for this moment. We have been busy, perhaps too busy. Maybe we ought to shed some of the load, for we are cluttered up with things; we become overwrought and tempers fray, there are so many things demanding our attention. Help us to get our priorities right. Some things can be left. Others - like this moment, we neglect at our peril. So, thank You for this quiet time of reflection and prayer. Help us to meditate on the pattern of our life.

Let us spend a moment in silent prayer that we might listen to God

We thank You, O God, for all high and holy things that touch our hearts, great music and literature, the solemn hush of a glorious evening when the clouds make golden islands in the west, for day is ending.
We give thanks for the memory of great moments – the thoughts of a childhood long past, our conversion, our wedding day - so many holy moments draw us to You again and Your love to us.

We thank You for those who have served us in love; when we were in need there were hearts to sympathise, and hands to help, and there were understanding minds - those in whom there was the sensitivity to Your Holy Spirit, and they ministered to us.
We were on holy ground - and we are now as we recollect them.

Help us, Father, never to despair of those whom the world writes off as failures - the 'drop-outs' of this world, the fallen, the weak who are easily led astray, give to us that sensitive heart to sorrow over them as though they belonged to us - our family, for indeed they do, as we live in Jesus.
We pray for them all. And grant us, Lord Jesus, the power to live beyond our means - we need Your strength, we need faith, above all, give us the sure confidence that there is always in our company, one whom we forget to count.

Hear us for Your Love's sake. **Amen.**

Remembering

O God, our Father, Creator of all that exists, sustainer of the Universe, yet Light of the lonely pilgrim's heart; beyond our highest thought, yet, Lover of our souls in Jesus, we come to You with praise and adoration.

We thank You, that in Jesus we see the very nature of Your heart. He came to show us Yourself, and give to us new life and hope, a joy that no man can take away from us, and a peace beyond our imagining.

Give to us, we pray, a clearer understanding of Your Word, help us to embrace its promises and to heed its warnings.

In the fellowship of Your Church, help us to continue to bear one another's burdens and build us up in love.

Let us pray for those who belong to us by ties of flesh and blood or by ties of the spirit.

Let us spend a moment remembering them.

We thank You, O Lord, that there is no place from which You are absent, that neither time or distance can separate us from Yourself, that those who are absent from us are still present with You.
Have in Your holy keeping, those whom we have remembered in prayer.

Let us pray for the homeless and refugees at this time.
Look in mercy, Father, upon all who suffer the lack of livelihood, and like Your beloved Son, have nowhere to lay their head.
You have assured us that those who do good to others, do it to Him, move our hearts to feel their misery, and to be generous in our giving to those agencies that are seeking to help lighten the burdens of the needy and distressed.

Comfort with Your presence, Lord Jesus, all who suffer this day, grant them relief from their pain, their anxiety.

And for ourselves, we pray: Forgive our sins, restore us again to Yourself that we may walk in peace and serve our fellows in love, for Your name's sake.

Amen.

The Seekers

Most Blessed God, we know that we were born seeking, men have always been looking for life and that which makes life worth living, but we know now, that You were seeking us with Your offer of life abundant - You sought, and You found us.
We were on the wrong road, wandering away and You spoke with us, "This is the Way, walk in it". And we found home, the home of our spirit. We knew, then, that we were made for fellowship with You.

Our hearts are full of gratitude, for we know that wherever we are there You are also.

We pray, Father, for those who are still seeking the one thing needful for victorious living – could they but know it they are often not far from the Kingdom of heaven, for the road to Yourself is as close as breathing, and nearer than hands or feet - a hurt conscience, asking forgiveness of another, a relationship restored, the sense of sin or of inadequacy.

Help all who need peace of heart and mind to find it in Jesus Christ.

Give to us, we pray, all that we need for our daily living - the trust that helps us to live one day at a time, and help us to live today well. Give us love - love for all men so that we will never misjudge them or attribute to them mean motives.

Give to us Your Holy Spirit's leading that we may be led aright, for we only want Your will for us, so shall we live the simple uncomplicated life.

Forgive us wanting our own way, for we are not wise, and by ourselves we wander from the path of truth, lead us, Lord, in the paths of righteousness.

Forgive us our un-loveliness, our lack of staying-power, fortify us by Your Spirit and enable us for all things.

Bless Your Church, keep us caring and keep us serving, may the mind that was in Jesus be in us also so that we see all men with a look of love.

Hear us for Your name's sake. **Amen.**

His Church

We give thanks our God and Father, for all the blessings that have enriched our lives and sustained us. Especially for the fellowship of Your Church, this holy and sacred mystery, spread throughout time and space, and rooted in eternity.

We thank You for the saints and martyrs of every age, and for those who, today stand fast in the faith amid tyranny and are persecuted for their belief. They challenge us, Father - challenge our apathy, our unadventurous living.

We praise You that in our generation there is a new understanding of Your purpose for the Church, the growth of respect of Christian communions for one another. We bless You for the prophets of today who have proclaimed Your power to heal divisions – the societies and movements that have broken down barriers, and for the younger Churches which have led the way.

We pray for the new Churches in Asia, and elsewhere, their native ministers and leaders, for the Spirit of Jesus is awakening men and women to newness of life.

Forgive us that sometimes we become despondent about the work in which we are engaged, it is because we lack the world vision, but Your Holy Spirit is moving in the hearts and minds of people throughout the world, and thousands - today, will come into the Kingdom in our land, and in South America, Korea and Africa.

Bless, we pray, all Churches labouring in our towns and cities, students from overseas in our colleges and universities, chaplains in hospitals, prisons and the educational field, those who serve among Her Majesty's Forces - and bless, Lord our minister and his family in this place. Keep us all serving, Lord Jesus, with love in our hearts for all.

Amen.

Keeping Things in Perspective

Almighty God, our heavenly Father, we are not worthy to be called Your children, for when light and darkness have been set before us we have often chosen darkness rather than light.

We were in an alien atmosphere - as Peter once was, and we denied You, and denied our discipleship. We didn't want to seem different, we were afraid of the company. We were tempted - and we fell.

Forgive us, Father, and help us in difficult situations, to know that You stand beside us with Your grace. Help us to see the weakness of falsehood and the strength of truth, the sinfulness of selfishness and the beauty of love and sacrifice.

Help us by Your Spirit to live with grace in our heart - to live in the morality of grace, for we have often found it easier to weep with those who weep than to rejoice with those who rejoice; the spirit of the elder brother in the parable has been in us also.

We have been niggardly in appreciation of someone else's success, been guilty of sins of the spirit, harboured resentment, been full of self-pity.

We have found it easier to pray for the poor than the affluent, but they too need our prayers, for wealth brings responsibilities.

Keep us growing in grace, Lord, that with the passing years we may enter more fully into the vastness of our faith.

We thank You that when distress comes upon us and our mortal schemes vanish into thin air, and our hearts are heavy, that someone is there to help us; someone shares our load - some human being whose heart is large and whose mind sees deeply - and the companionship is none other than Yours.

Hear our prayer, O God, for we ask it in the Saviour's name.

Amen.

Right Perspective

O God, our Father, it is good to be here in this place where our spirits can know peace - this place where we get things into their right perspective.

Life seems so distorted at times, and events are so near to us that we cannot take the long view. Help us to know that You have set us within the framework of eternity, and our lives can never be satisfied with the trivial.

We thank You for the quietness which enables us to hear Your voice - and our readiness, now, to listen.

Forgive us, we pray, that we are bungling instruments in Your Kingdom, impatient when things do not go our way, and when they do, it is not always the right way.

Teach us to know when the Holy Spirit is speaking with us, then to follow His leading at whatever cost to ourselves.

Help us, we pray, to walk this week among men and women as those who have been in this place today - peace in our hearts, at one with You, ourselves and all folk everywhere, and where there is discord, help us to be reconcilers.

Give to us the adventuring spirit in our daily living. Open up for us avenues of friendship, help us to make new friends - and if we have neglected old ones, help us to make amends. But, above all, help us to know the friendship of Jesus, wherever we walk, and wherever we go.

We pray, Father, for the friendless, and for those who find it hard to make friends - the shy and self-conscious, for the stranger in the large city, and the student away from home.

Bless those who are lonely because of bereavement, whom the neighbours soon forget after the funeral.
 Those working in other lands who miss home and family.
 Those who are lonely because of a guilty conscience and they cannot find peace.
 Embrace them all, we pray, in Your love - and us too Father, for Your Son, our Saviour's sake.

Amen.

Give Us Power Lord

O Eternal God, in fellowship with You is our peace, and in this place today, we come apart from the world of things and our pre-occupation with its many tasks to seek peace and power and insight that we may live adequately.

We confess, O God, that there is not much about our life that is radiant, nor have we done much to further the Kingdom among men. Jesus said, *"Greater things shall you do ..."* but we haven't the power.

Give us power Lord, help us to live beyond our meagre resources - give us Yourself. Help us to surrender that inner citadel to You, so shall we know how to live abundantly.

We thank You, Father, for Jesus, and for the assurance that He gave us that You are ever working to draw men and women to Yourself.

Help us to see that apart from the enabling power of Your Holy Spirit our serving is vain, but with Him dwelling in these temples of ours, we speak a divine love, not only with our lips, but in our lives.

Hear our prayers, O God, for all upon whom the trials of life press heavily:
For those who suffer because of others' sins. Sustain those noble fathers and mothers who bear the burdens of their erring children. Give strength to the weak, hope to those whose faith is flickering in the last few drops of oil, and courage to those who are burdened with physical suffering and infirmity, and feel themselves to be of little use. Teach them that by their faith and patience they may serve You still by the grace that is made perfect in weakness.

Help us to always bear one another's burdens and so fulfil the law of Christ. Use us as vessels of Your grace, may Your love flow through us to others in helpful service and good fellowship, to the glory of Your Holy name, through Christ our Lord.

Amen.

You Believe In Us

O God, our Father, You have given us life and set before us a life to live in Your world and given us an appetite for the true, the lovely and the worthwhile.

Within our hearts there is a hunger for eternal things, and You sent Your Son Jesus Christ that we may know the reality of the spiritual. You know us altogether, the innermost thoughts of our hearts, our longings and aspirations.

We confess our failures, Father - our failures in love, for we often fail to trust You, we are apprehensive when we face an unexpected problem. We have moments when we despair of ourselves, we seem always to fail.

Help us, then, to know that You believe in us, and that with You, all things are possible.

We give thanks O God for Your forgiveness, a new start, and a sense of peace within us. Our hearts are glad and truly thankful that You love us, we do have a faith to believe and a Saviour to trust, and Your Holy Spirit to lead us, and the fellowship of Your people here, where we bear one another's burdens.

Bless, we pray, those who find themselves in difficulty, grant them light upon their problem, that they may see the way ahead. Release into freedom, Father, those who are in bondage to fears, fears known and unknown. Those whose bodies have broken down, grant them healing, and those whose minds will not let them know peace because of what they have done - or failed to do. Where there is estrangement, help them to become reconciled, where there is a sense of guilt, lead them to ask Your forgiveness, and feel the reality of it.

Give us a deeper concern for our fellows, Lord. Help us to sit where they sit, that we may understand, and help.

Hear us, for Jesus Christ's sake.

Amen.

Sight and Insight

O God, our Father, Creator of all that is, and by whom they are sustained and nurtured, we, Your children come and give thanks for all Your goodness to us.

We give thanks for the world in which we live. The world of nature which ministers to our physical needs, and the need of our eyes for loveliness, in forest and field, mountain and dale, sea and stream to cheer our hearts and rest our town-tired eyes.

We thank You for the world of the spirit that ministers to our need of the true, the good and the holy. For all gracious thoughts, and all lovely actions that inspire us. We give thanks for sight and insight, and Your Holy Spirit's touch upon our souls.

We rejoice in the Christian experience of Your redeeming love in Jesus, Your forgiveness when we have spoiled our life - or spoiled another's. We ask forgiveness, now, for any action of ours that this past week has denied our faith, the things we have done that were unworthy. And things of the spirit, of which we alone are conscious - but You know - You know us altogether, every thought of our heart.

Help us, O God, to handle our lives adequately in difficult situations. In times of testing, throw around us Your protecting grace, for temptations are not always in front of us, they are at the back of our mind. Give us victory, then, in Jesus.

We pray, Father, for all who are finding life hard - those who are haunted by doubts, help them to certainty. All who are depressed by failure and disappointment, help them to take heart and begin again.

And in this hour of worship, in Your mercy, heal us all.

Hear us, for Jesus Christ's sake.

Amen.

Freedom

Let us, in silence, bring our thanks to God for our own particular blessings.

Period of silence

> For the joy of this day.
>
> For the truth of the Word.
>
> For the promise of Christ's presence.
>
> For the peace that passes knowledge.
>
> For the fellowship that here we find.
>
> For all that Christian experience means to us.

We thank You, Father. Give us grace in this hour to appropriate all that You offer to us, through Jesus Christ, our Lord.

We bless Your Holy name for the freedom that is ours in Jesus, once we were in bondage to ourselves, and now we are free - free to do as we ought, and we find it no binding restriction, for our whole desire is to do the right; duty is no hard word for Your love is in our hearts.

We are free from the imprisoning nature of the crowd - what people will say and what they will think about us, so insinuations cannot hurt us. We are free to serve our fellows with glad hearts, and with all that we have and are.

We give thanks for Your Spirit's leading, we have trodden ways that were Divinely directed – of that we are sure. Many things have been ours, not because we deserved them, or sought them, but You prepared them for us.

Give us, we pray, that sensitive spirit that responds to the influence of the Divine, help us to know when You are speaking with us, to distinguish between our will and Yours, and then to act upon it.

We pray, Father for men and women in all their lostness. You are waiting to be gracious still, and full of compassion. We commend them to You now - the known and the unknown.

In Your mercy heal us all, for Jesus Christ's sake.

Amen.

The Trusting Heart of Childhood

Most gracious God, we thank You for all that we receive at Your hand day by day. For the gift of life itself, for reason and conscience, for nurture and guidance - for all the gifts of nature and grace; for Your forbearance and Your tender mercies that never fail, despite our sinning.

We come, Father, knowing that it is Your nature always to give, so we come asking as a child asks of those who love him.

We ask forgiveness for all that has spoiled our relationship with You, we are aware of where we have failed. Forgive us Lord, we are truly sorry, renew a right spirit within us, that we may start again.

Give to us, we pray, the trusting heart of childhood. Give to us the simplicity that once we knew. Untangle our complicated lives, and help us live the guided life, to obey the leading of Your Holy Spirit.

Help us to know Your will for us, and to do the Christlike thing, not asking where it may lead, content to obey and leave the outcome with You.

Fill us with Your Spirit, Lord. Give us joy in believing and the singing heart and send us on our way rejoicing.

And hear us Father, as we pray for Your needy children everywhere. For those seeking a faith to believe in a world of confused voices. Help them to hear the still small voice that whispers 'come' - come home, there is rest for your weariness, a peace that the world can never give, or ever take away, and power for living.

In Your mercy, bless all who need the comfort and healing of Jesus. Hear us, for His sake.

Amen.

Thank You, Lord for forgiveness. Help us to accept it, and enable us to forgive ourselves, let Your pardoning of our failures be sufficient for us, so shall we know that inner peace and begin again, free from every stain of the past.

Give us the power to conquer inbred sin, our pride, our prejudices, our self-sufficiency.

Write Your law of love upon our hearts.

This we ask in Jesus' name. **Amen.**

MOORLEYS

We are growing publishers, adding several new titles to our list each year. We also undertake private publications and commissioned works.

Our range includes:-

Books of Verse:
Devotional Poetry
Recitations for Children
Humorous Monologues

Drama
Bible Plays
Sketches
Christmas, Passiontide,
  Easter and Harvest Plays
Demonstrations

Resource Books
Assembly Material
Songs and Musicals
Children's Addresses
Prayers
Worship and Preaching
Books for Speakers

Activity Books
Quizzes
Puzzles
Painting Books

Church Stationery
Notice Books
Cradle Roll Certificates
Presentation Labels

Associated Lists and Imprints
Cliff College Publishing
Nimbus Press
Headway
Social Workers Christian Fellowship

Please send a stamped addressed envelope (C5 approx 9" x 6") for the current catalogue or consult your local Christian Bookshop who will either stock or be able to obtain Moorleys titles.